Crochet Me a Life

This short collection of poems was written between March 2020 and August 2023.

I wanted to reflect on the emotions we have all been dealing with during these tumultuous times and perhaps make you smile at all the crazy things we did to keep sane during the Covid lockdowns. The places mentioned in the poems are very precious to me and I want to thank all the hard-working folk who keep our special pubs and cafes open to enable the magic to go on happening, you know who you are and I love you all.

Sue Thompson
August 2023

List of Titles:

Lockdown poems
Me and the bees and the trees
Lopsided
Who Cares
Musically Inspired poems
The Ukulele Player
Kate the Cake Lady
The Music Man
Sing for Joy
I'll Stop Now
Sweffling White Horse poems
Where's Sweffling
Pubbub
The tattooed lady
Mat's poem
Authorly observations
The Fronted Adverbial
Wordle
Tinkerbell
Princess Diana's Angry Ghost
The Bookshop Lament
Poems for Strange Times
The Invitation

Emotional Wreckage

The Angel

The 2022 Song

Dazed and Confused

Crackers

Dessert

Doughnuts

Lost in Translation

The Christmas Onesie

The Lady with the Scarf

Crochet me a life

Smile

Rants

The Gazebo Poem

Road Rage

Lockdown Poems

These three poems were written during the spring lockdown when we were all trying to come to terms with the isolation imposed on us by Covid 19. I found this particularly hard as I lived in a remote village and am not comfortable with technology but I found solace in our beautiful Suffolk countryside and comfort as always in words.

The first poem came to me on one of my long solitary walks during the beautiful weather of that quiet time. The only sound made was the regular slap of my sandals and the hum of bees and insects and my only company my own thoughts and fears.

Me and the Bees and the Trees

My sandals slap on dusty roads
the only sound I hear.
Butterflies swoop through banks of flowers
in the greening fields there are deer.
Then I walk for miles to free my mind
from thoughts of feared disease
down quiet lanes, through a tunnel of green
just me and the bees and the trees.

It's getting hotter every day
the farmers long for rain.
Tractors toil through clouds of dust
as I walk alone again.
I haven't seen my family
since snow was on the ground
my friends a distant memory
they mustn't come around.
We used to sing together
now I hear them on my phone
the songs are still the same
but we're all singing on our own.

Now I walk to keep my sanity
through waves of dust and heat
and mostly I feel happy
to be healthy and complete
surrounded by the birdsong
I never heard before

I join them in my head
til I'm not lonely anymore.

***

Who Cares was written for a lovely man who lives in a remote part of Suffolk with no internet connection. He sits in the same spot every night at the Sweffling White Horse and when lockdown closed the pub we feared he would be lonely.

The landlady of the pub came up with the idea of delivering beer to him on her bicycle and leaving it outside his door with letters and verses from his friends to cheer him up.
 Now that the pub has reopened he has resumed his rightful place and life is good once more.

Who Cares

Who cares if your hair turns grey?
Who cares if you've washed today?
Who cares if your clothes are clean?
Who cares if you live on beans?

Sit in the garden,
watch the bees.
Don't mow your lawn
or trim your trees.
Read a book,
drink more beer.
Don't turn on the news
it's too sad to hear.

Write a novel.
Take up sport.
But don't have a party
you might get caught
by the Covid Police
they know your sort.
But…
Who cares if you dance all night
on your own
out of sight?
Sing if you want to
make a din.
This isolation's not such a bad thing.

***

One of the many new skills I adopted during the first lockdown, along with extreme cleaning and colour coding all my books and clothes, was home hairdressing. This occupation was very popular in our village and by June we were peering at unrecognisable old friends from the mandatory two meters apart and wondering who on earth we had become.

Lopsided

Have you lopped off your locks during lockdown?
Though I swore that I wouldn't give in
it's been seventeen weeks
now I look like a freak.
It's caused me to break out the gin.

I found me some scissors to work with
they've been handy for toenails and string.
I'm sure when it comes to my straggly mop
they'll turn out to be just the thing.

I looked at tutorials on YouTube.
"Don't cut it wet" they all said.
"Chop into the hair but remember, take care
not to chop up your eyeballs instead".

These scissors are terribly pointy
but I've started so best carry on.
I won't tackle the back
just my long fringe to hack
oh help, where've the plasters all gone?

Well, my eyeballs remain where they should be
but I can't say the same for my hair
it still hangs round my face
and it looks a disgrace
I'm riddled with shame and despair.

I'm going to the hairdresser shortly
with my mask, and my apron and gown.
On the twenty sixth day of July
at mid-day
then I'll be the talk of the town.

***

Musical Musings

I tend to spend a lot of time in small tucked away Suffolk pubs singing with groups of friends. We sing all the old songs we love, unfashionable and probably politically incorrect ballads like Delilah or Lucille, but we have a lot of fun and it makes me very happy.

I hope you enjoy reading these verses as much as I enjoyed writing them.

My husband has seven ukuleles. He bought another one when we took a trip to Ipswich recently to take pictures of the Owl Trail, and for me to buy more books. Buying books is therapy. Buying ukuleles is a criminal offence.

His excuse was that he liked the colour (Dragon Fruit, or purple to you and me). I rest my case.

This poem is for all the long-suffering ukulele wives out there, I feel your pain.

The Ukulele Player

The ukulele player is a jolly sort of chap.
He likes his songs traditional,
he doesn't care for rap.
He's got no time for Eminem
Jay Zee or Kurtis Blow
Run DMC or Dr Drey.
He'd tell them where to go.

He's fond of a sea shanty
or a merry Irish jig.
Something to make you tap your feet
as at your beer you swig.

He doesn't mind if you join in
or if you're out of tune
and if you should forget the words
just tap it with your spoon.

He likes to jam along with friends
who meet him in the pub
the Castle or the Blaxhall Ship
at these he is the hub.
He'll play folk, blues or country
he'll even do requests.
"Over the hills and far away" is the one they like the best.

But the ukulele player has ambition to succeed.
He's got more ukuleles than a man would ever need.

So if you want an artist to perform at your big day
call the ukulele player, and he'll be round
right away.

***

I have a lovely friend called Kate who is a very important part of our happy singing group known as the Fram Friends. We meet on the second and fourth Tuesday of each month in the events room of the Castle Inn which sits proudly next to Ed's castle on the hill in Framlingham.

Kate makes amazing cakes and usually shows up with her latest delights in large boxes for us to try, we are her guinea pigs, or maybe just pigs, eager to sample the goods.
I wrote this verse as a thank you for the joy Kate brings into our sad cakeless lives. I'm sure it's good for our health.

Kate the Cake Lady

Oh Kate the cake lady
see what you have done
my waistline's expanded
my jeans are undone
my mouth's smeared with chocolate
my face is a mess
I've crumbs round my chin
and I need a new dress.

What joy when we see you
opening the door
with a box in each hand
and the promise of more.
Will it be lemon drizzle, jam sponge or a pie?
I've no will-power
I'm weak.
It's Black Forest or die.

Oh Kate the cake lady
you're bad for my diet
what's that in the box?
I'm impatient to try it.
I'll be your guinea pig
this is my fate
so here's to more singing
and putting on weight.

I wrote this next poem for a very special man named John Ward who, together with his wife Lynne, has been entertaining us for many years in our favourite musical haunts.

He can hold an audience spellbound for hours with his singing and playing, there doesn't seem to be a song he can't perform and he loves it when we join in.

John has the ability to lift the spirits when you are feeling low, he writes songs of hope and joy that are timeless.

The Music Man

In the Blaxhall Ship at three o'clock
the music man will play.
His joyful songs of hope and cheer
will chase all cares away.
Nobody here is lonely
nobody here is poor
all our fears and sorrows
we leave outside the door.
The cold wind shakes the windows
but inside we are snug
the music and the singing
wrap us warmly, like a hug.

He plays the songs we love to sing
the ones that we all know
like a fabled troubadour
from days of long ago.

**

I was asked by my Fram Friends singing group to write a poem illustrating what we were about in order to encourage new people to join the group. Our meetings are a highlight of my social life so I was eager to share the joy with others, and thankfully the Friends approved of my effort.

I would encourage anyone looking to put some fun into their life to search out a singing group, you meet some great people too.

Sing for Joy

Sing for joy, sing together
gather round, all join in.
Never mind if your memory fails you
we'll help out once you begin.

We have Banjo Brian in the corner
no matter what, he'll carry on
Maggie May is captured by another Brian,
a lively lady to Australia gone.
Pete sings of Silkies with his ukulele
kind Kate brings cakes and a soldiers' song.
If John were a carpenter he'd find his lady.
Bob would play his ukulele as the ship goes down.

Here are Nick and Margaret to entertain us
with summery songs to make us smile.
A lovely day is always forecast,
no more rainclouds for a while.

Gerry plays clarinet so sweetly.
Sue writes poems (so they say)
We gather round the old grey castle
voices raised on a happy day.

So sing for joy, sing together.
No judgement here, no unkind word.
All are friends joined by the music,
freed from care, free as a bird.

***

Sweffling White Horse Poems

The White Horse pub in Sweffling is my happy place, everyone should have one, a place to go where you just fit, where your favourite people are always to be found and no matter how low you feel or how sad the world, you know you are accepted and everything will be ok.
I've already written two books featuring goings on in Sweffling but the inspiration and crazy events keep occurring so here's some more Sweffling mayhem for you to enjoy.

The lovely landlady of the White Horse is called Maz and her favourite sound is the lively hum of conversation rising from the pub on busy nights, or more usually during the rowdy Sunday lunchtime sessions when we all put the world to rights. This can take some time but the arguments, however strongly fought, are always put aside when we leave, to be resumed the following Sunday with gusto. Maz calls this sound "pubbub", a great word and one we have now all adopted.

Pubbub

Our local is a happy place
A jolly little spot.
It's safe to say we like it here,
we like it here a lot.

There's comfort in the cushions
music soaked into the walls.
There's pubbub round snug tables
as deep country darkness falls.

It gets busy Sunday lunchtimes
when we put the world to rights.
Rubbish telly, politicians ,
we've got them in our sights.

As we wolf down our cheese toasties
call for more ale in our pot
it's safe to say we like it here,
we like it here a lot.

One of the joys of visiting the White Horse is meeting fascinating new people.
There is a small campsite behind the pub which attracts campers of the eccentric persuasion and memorable faces appear in the pub to liven up proceedings on a rare quiet night.

One such person was a very beautiful young lady who attracted a lot of attention due to the unusual tattoo on her upper arm. It was an upright hoover, a little like the one featured in that brilliant video accompanying Queen's song "I want to break free".

The lady explained that she was a fan of hoovers, as I said you meet all sorts at the Sweffling White Horse, and I was so impressed I promised her a poem in honour of her tattoo. This is it.

The Tattooed Lady

I met a lady with a hoover
tattooed on her arm.
A tattoo of a hoover wouldn't do you any harm.
Unlike a skull and crossbones
which could cause your nerves to jangle.
I'd much prefer a hoover,
or a saucepan,
or a mangle.

We discovered the Sweffling White Horse on a charity walk in 2016 to raise money for the Brain Tumour Charity.

Our wonderful friend Mat Bayfield, who suffered from this terrible disease, organised many walks around Suffolk's towns and villages and in doing so raised tens of thousands of pounds for the charity. Sadly, by the end of 2018 he was accompanying us in a wheelchair and in October 2019 he died.

Mat was one of the most inspirational people I have ever met, we all miss him and his huge presence in the pub.

Sometimes on a lively night, when someone takes up a guitar and starts to play and we all join in, I can still hear him belting out a tune, the centre of laughter and merriment.

I wrote this poem after a magical evening when a campsite visitor brought out his guitar and played "The Wild Rover". It made the hairs on my arms stand up, as if a ghost were playing along with us.

Mat's Poem

It's the feeling, it's the feeling
It's the shiver on my skin.
It's the open door on a warm dark night
as the music draws you in.
By the dartboard in the corner
where you used to sing so clear
another voice is singing
but it's your voice I can hear.

It's the joy on all the faces
as they raise their voice in song.
It's the pounding on the tables
echoing a beat so strong.
It's the soaring of our spirits
the feeling of release
the sound of carefree laughter
the happiness, the peace.

It's the memories we are sharing
with the ones who knew you best
that rise up when we gather
in the place your spirit rests.
And as the night is falling
at the closing of the day
we all know, who love and miss you
that you haven't gone away.

Writery Thoughts

As a writer I am always on the lookout for new trends in grammar and vocabulary to amuse and impress my reader, and in one of my numerous late night conversations with Dr Google I came across the fronted adverbial.

I had been using these tricky little customers for years without realising I was a trend-setter. Imagine my joy when I came across a giant poster, complete with eye-catching illustrations and listing clever examples of the new grammatical star stuck on a wall in the Aldeburgh Bookshop.

I hurried home and quickly penned this homage to the writers' new best friend.

The Fronted Adverbial

I am a fronted adverbial.
Sometimes I blankly stare.
Without warning, in the distance,
quite understandably, I despair
Nobody understands me.
I'm not easy to explain.
Sometimes I like to imagine
I'm a noun, a full stop, or a train.

Tomorrow, I think I will be something else
a change of career, that's the ticket.
Without a sound, joyfully, when the rain stops
I'll check out my options and pick it.

***

In common with many of my friends who really should know better my first action on waking at silly o' clock on a midsummer morning is to turn on my phone and click onto Wordle.

We all do it. Some of us even post our results online (boasting) and although I haven't mastered this yet if I have a good day I do brag about it on Facebook.

A two day is sprinkled with stardust, a six and I might stay in bed. We won't talk about those terrible days when I don't get it at all. I wrote the following for fellow sufferers.

Wordle

Sweet Mary and Joseph
that isn't a word
that's not how you spell it
this game is absurd.
That must be a trade-name.
That's cheating, what rot.
I'm finished, not playing
and happy I'm not.

You got it in three?
Well bully for you
the world hates a show-off
I certainly do.

I'm coming off FaceBook as soon as I'm done
Oh, hang on, it's "Natal",
in six though, oh bum!

I've been here an hour now
scratching my head.
Oh why can't I get it?
I'm very well read.
I've got my thesaurus
dog-eared and well thumbed
and my fat Collins Dictionary's depths have been plumbed.

I dread every morning I click on to see
this fearful conundrum unfold before me.
But I won't be defeated
my new starter word
will be my salvation
now "water" or "third"?

***

This is my author's rant, everything described in my poem happened to me and similar horrible things have been said to other writers I have spoken to.

It's hard getting your work acknowledged but I love writing, it brings me joy and I want to share it. But not everyone loves reading, as I have found out to my cost.

I called my rant "Tinkerbell" after the fairy in Peter Pan who said that every time someone declares "I don't believe in fairies" another fairy dies. Please be nice to authors, a kind word can make our day.

Tinkerbell

Last month I joined a Whatsapp group
for people who love books,
fans of gorgeous gardens
and recipes, for cooks.
I felt a glow of welcome
these people were my tribe
as I posted pictures of my books
so they could feel the vibe.
But then…

"I don't read books."
Those cruel words
that cut you down to size.
"I don't have time".
Somewhere, unseen, another author dies.
That tiny comment from a stranger
sparked off memories sad
of thoughtless words from unkind lips
that drive an author mad.
The worst ones show some interest
until they see the price
"Is that each book?" they gasp
as if they can't believe their eyes.
"I buy books cheap in Tesco
when I get my beer and pies".
Somewhere unpaid, unrecognised
another author dies.

"My mother used to read"
they sometimes say
"but when she died we gave her books away.
We haven't got the time, the urge, the space
your little book would clutter up the place".
Then off they go for burgers and French fries.
Unmourned, unread, another author dies.

With hopeful stride and bag of books
I step into the shop.
I scour the shelves for copies,
don't let it be a flop.
There's just one left
where I left six
oh joy, will he take more?
The busy harassed bookseller regards me
 from the floor.
"You've only got one left" I say
"Can I leave these today?"
He peers at me, emotionless
my heart is pounding low
after an endless pause he speaks
"I think we'll call that no."
Then with my shameful, downcast face
I take my books and go.

I didn't get an order
I won't collect the prize.
Dejected and rejected now
another author dies.
I've just received an email
would I like to give a talk
on authorly activities
it's only a short walk

down to my local library
where friendly readers go
twenty eight good souls turn up
the smiles and questions flow.
They buy some books (hooray!)
I'm later told
my talk was a success
and other libraries want to know
if I will be their guest.
I keep a little notebook
to record each one who buys
for every time their book is read
another author flies.

**

I am a proud member of the Suffolk Writers' Group, a bunch of hugely supportive people who offer advice and help to each other in all things to do with writing and publishing work. The group is led by a very talented writer called Mai Black who has published a book called "Thirty Angry Ghosts".

The poems are written from the point of view of historical figures such as Shakespeare and Queen Victoria who have good reason to be angry at the way history has treated them. I would highly recommend this book, it is educational as well as amusing as Mai has included short biographies of each character at the end of the book.

Mai holds competitions to encourage the group to try new things and recently she challenged us to write our own angry ghost poem choosing our own ghostly character. I have always felt that Princess Diana was treated very cruelly at an age when she should have been developing a sense of judgement, so this is my imagination of her point of view from the grave.

Princess Diana's Angry Ghost

I was sweet sixteen when I fell in love
not with an innocent boy
a playground crush
the boy next door
but with an adult man
near twice my age
a royal Prince
already deep in love.

But not with me,
never with me.

Aged nineteen,
dazzled by my engagement sapphire
surrounded by diamonds,
chosen by me to match my eyes
my shining bright blue eyes.
Shy and awkward in a smart blue suit
with fashionable white ruffled blouse
too old for me, so staid.
My eyes cast down
facing my impending marriage
with childlike, heartbreaking joy.

When asked what he recalled of his first sight of me
my Prince replied " A very jolly, amusing and attractive sixteen year old".
"Very jolly"? Am I your pigtailed niece?
Your drunken uncle?
"Amusing"?
Where were the thunderbolts, the flash of desire?
"Enchanting, intoxicating, ravishing"
 these are words to herald the love of your life.
But no, he had met her long ago.
"Amusing" is what you call your cat.

But reader, I married him.
Gave him two fine sons,
an heir, a spare.
Respectability, the approval of his family,
the adulation and admiration of his public
for his beautiful young wife.
Space to be with her, his real love.

Now I watch from my cold and lonely grave.
See them happy, married, content
beside my grown sons with their stylish wives,
one wearing my dazzling ring.
At least it was bestowed with love.
Five adorable grandchildren surround you.
They should be in my arms.
My cold, empty arms.

When you stand upon that balcony
with her, in all your finery
look behind you, lover.
I am not amusing now.

***

This poem is dedicated to all our wonderful independent bookshops which are at present struggling to survive against the likes of Amazon and the supermarket discounting of books.

In particular I would like to thank the unique and enthusiastic supporter of local authors Andrew Marsh of Dial Lane Books in Ipswich. He stocks my books, promotes them online and holds events featuring local authors who sign their books and talk to readers in his amazing shop. In fact Andrew has an entire area in his shop dedicated to local authors including many of the Suffolk Writers Group.
He also has a framed copy of The Bookshop Lament on his wall in the shop. This makes me very happy.

The Bookshop Lament

I'll only be a minute, you needn't park and pay.
He's put my book aside, I'll pick it up and leave
OK?

I won't browse round the shelves for something new, but if I did…
you'd better put three hours in the meter
here's five quid.

***

Poems for our strange times

You couldn't make it up could you? One pandemic, three prime ministers, one European war, one cost of living crisis, countless strikes and political scandals, Mat Hancock in the jungle and the death of our Queen in her platinum jubilee year.

I was tempted to hide under the quilt but instead I wrote a series of daft verses in an attempt to record it all.

I will be shaking my head as I type and murmuring "I do not believe it!"

In my previous book, Spending a Penny in Southwold, I included a story I made up at the start of the pandemic to take my mind off the horror unfolding each day. In this piece I poked fun at the incredible names chosen by Jacob Rees-Mogg for his unfortunate children. Look them up, you will not believe it.

I then suggested names for future mini Moggs. This went down a storm when I performed it at storytelling events so I wrote a verse to go with it in which I imagined Boris Johnson hearing of my story and calling me up to Downing Street to include me in the honours list. Baroness Thompson does have a certain ring.

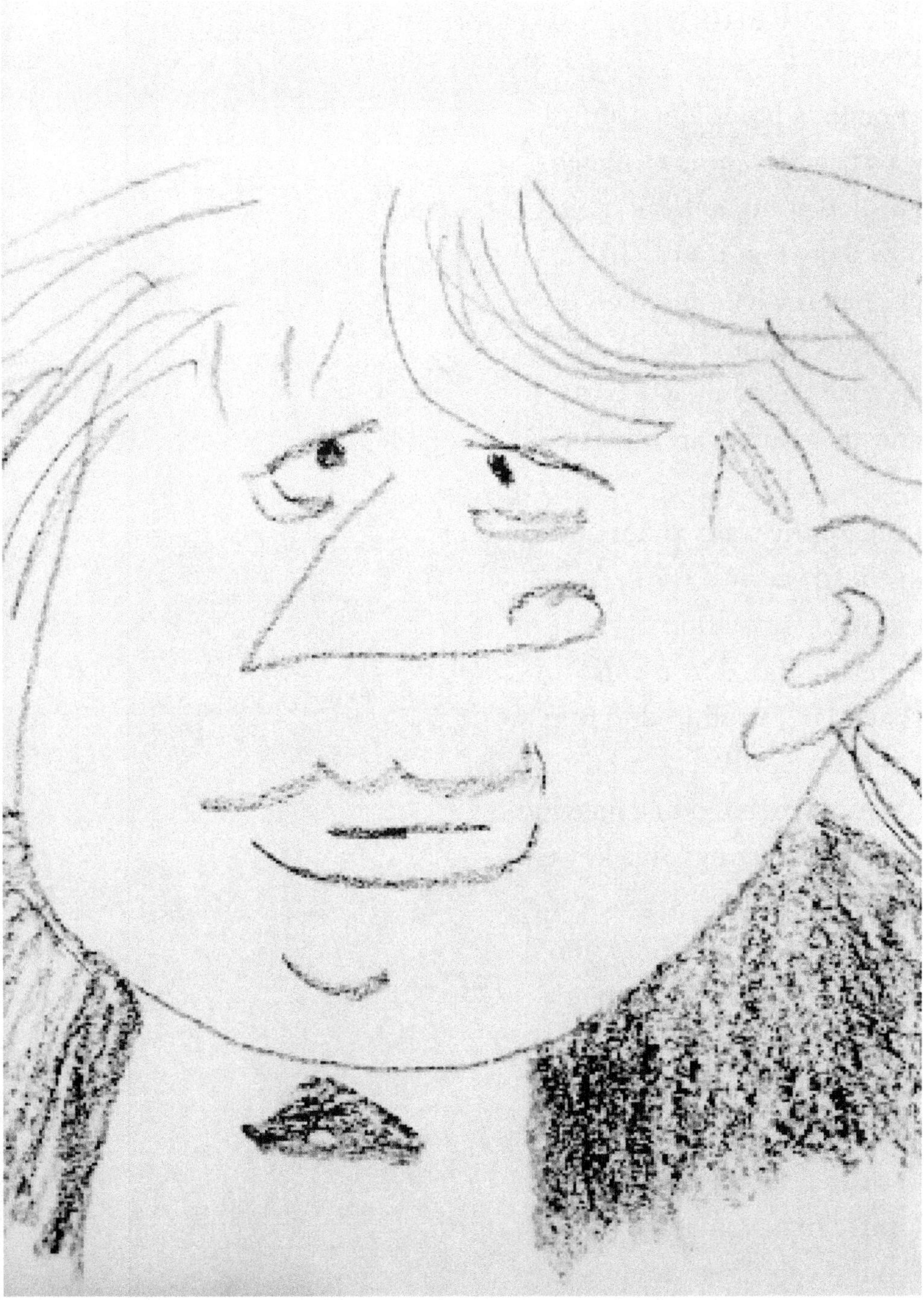

The Invitation

I bought a brand new outfit
with bag and shoes to match.
I peered at my reflection
now don't I look a catch?
I've had my hair and nails done
must do Suffolk proud
because I'm going to a party
now that parties are allowed.

I caught the train to London
my head was in a spin
I took my invitation
to ensure they'd let me in.
When I'm introduced to Boris
I'm sure he will be wowed
because I'm going to a meeting
now that meetings are allowed.

But when I stood before him
Boris' face fell in a frown.
He rubbed his chin, he scratched his head
he looked me up and down.
Then his eyes lit up, he shook his head
to clear away the fog.
"You're that woman who writes stories
about Jacob Rees-Mogg.

Now is the time to celebrate
my rapid rise to fame
forget pop stars and royalty
they're calling out MY name.

I've invited all the neighbours
I'm drumming up a crowd
because we're going to have a party
now that parties are allowed.

***

In a desperate attempt to cheer myself up after unwisely watching the early evening news I decided to watch the Eurovision Song Contest. I hadn't seen it for years, but I was in the mood for several hours of mindless idiocy and so settled back on my comfy sofa with a large glass of red and a packet of crisps.

Three hours later the glass and crisp packet were empty and I was an emotional wreck. I'd laughed, I'd danced and finally, when Ukraine won, I was blubbering for all I was worth.

I then realised that most of the last few years has felt like that, an emotional rollercoaster none of us could have prepared for. We need to let it out folks, so come on, blub along with me.

Emotional Wreckage

Anyone here can't stop crying?
Are you an emotional wreck?
I find as I go through these strangest of years
I can't keep my feelings in check.

The sight of Her Majesty smiling.
The terrible news from Ukraine.
A man with long hair singing "Spaceman"
and I reach for the tissues, again.

I used to be stiff upper lip-ed
in tragedy's face up I'd man.
Now I have to confess I'm a blubbering mess
as a Stoic I've gone down the pan.

Oh, don't take me to see a sad movie
the one where the little dog dies.
I may turn out to be that old cliché
the embarrassing woman who cries.

***

Emotional Wreckage

I feel this next piece belongs in this part of my book because although not a poem it expresses the sheer surreal horror of the events of 2022. Even though we were seeing the Ukraine war unfolding on the news every night, and it was almost unbearable to watch, it was not until I came face to face with the consequences in of all places quiet sleepy Hollesley that it really hit me what human beings are capable of, for good and bad.

My story was published in March 2023 on Instagram by Fiveminutelit who publish micro memoirs. I send pieces in regularly, it's great fun and good practice in condensing my thoughts.

The Angel

"How much is your little angel?" It was the last one on my craft stall, lovingly made with beads and wire. "It's a pound". I looked at my frail elderly customer, juggling her shopping bags. "I'll buy it for my friend who's staying with me, to protect her".

I thought of her friend, perhaps sick and left at home, as I tenderly wrapped the angel in tissue paper and handed it to the lady. "Ah, here she is now", and I looked up to see the friend. "Hello" she said quietly, shyly. A tall girl, elegant, young, smiling, beautiful, Ukranian.

***

Twenty twenty two really was a year to remember for all the wrong reasons. You couldn't make it up. It just went on and on, disaster after disaster and by June I was so fed up with it I decided to write a musical rant to get it out of my system.

 I even considered adding new verses every time another disaster occurred but quite honestly there is only so much you can take so I missed a few out. It is still a pretty long song though.

This should be sung with gusto to the tune of "There is nothing like a dame". If you know anyone who can accompany you boisterously on the piano it will sound better.

The 2022 song was written to be performed during the celebrations held for the Queen's Platinum Jubilee in June, it proved very popular but a lot of celebratory drinks had been consumed by the time I staggered to the mic to perform it.

The 2022 Song

We've had pestilence and war
we've has crises galore
we've had Currygate and Partygate
can't take it any more
we had monkey pox and covid
and the weather wasn't great
out comes the sun
and we all cremate.

This is 2022
what a year it's been
but the Jubilee's in June
so thank God we have the Queen.
I'm too scared to watch the news
see me shaking in my shoes
with the cost of living crisis
can't afford to drink or booze.
We've got Rootin' Tootin' Putin
and his psychopathic chums
they can take their nukes
and stick 'em up their bums.

We've got nothing to take off our horrid covid masks for.
The pubs and caffs are all closed cos they can't get any staff for…
This is 2022, what a year it's been
and it's only half way through
so thank God we have the Queen.

We had Boris, now he's gone
or at least he will be soon
won't be long til they replace him
with some other hopeless goon.
Oh, I don't know why they bother
might as well have you or me
we're not much good
but at least we're free.

This is 2022
what a year it's been
and there's still five months to go
so thank God we've got the Queen.

Well, the gloom goes on and on
now Her Majesty is gone
we all sat and watched the funeral
felt sad and lost and glum.
Now all we have is Charles and HER
however will it end?

When will there be some happy news?
Don't hold your breath my friend.

This is 2022, it's not over yet.
Now we've got Therese and Liz
It's as bad as it can get.

We had Kwasi, now he's gone
well he wasn't here for long
now we seem to have some man called Hunt
whatever could go wrong?
If they're all still here at Christmas
then I'm going to eat my hat
the only ones with staying power
are Boris and the cat.

Things have finally settled down
good ole Rishi's back in town
with his firm hand on the tiller
so we don't all up and drown.
But can he outlast a lettuce
or will his charisma wilt?
I've finally stopped caring
gonna hide under the quilt.

Its still 2022
still two months to go
Halloween and Christmas loom
bringing doom and gloom and snow.

Now I'm sitting watching telly
and I can't believe my eyes
there's Matt Hancock in the Jungle
with the snakes and rats and flies.
Did you hear COP 27 say we're all about to fry?
No post, no trains no nurses
it's enough to make you cry.

There's no eggs or sprouts or lettuces or turkey.
Don't leave the house whatever you do or you might get the lurgy.

That was 2022
Glad it's nearly gone
looking forward to next year
full of wine and fun and song.

***

We went on a ten day holiday to Fuertaventura in January. It was the first time we had been away in winter and also our first experience of staying in a hotel on a half-board basis.

I can't say it was all good, or even mostly good, but it certainly encouraged the creative flow as during this time I wrote five new poems inspired by our adventures. As this probably works out to around £200 per poem I think I'll now go back to writing about Suffolk.

Dazed and Confused

I'm dazed and confused in Departures
my Kindle is in the wrong case
my liquids are not in a clear plastic bag
my brain is all over the place.

I didn't get lost in the car park
I didn't forget where to go
but I managed to look like a dingbat
it's my forte in case you don't know.

***

The next two poems are about my love of food, I list greed and gluttony as my favourite vices and if you have ever been on an all-inclusive holiday this should strike a chord. It shouldn't be allowed, but I'm very glad it is. Someone told me you arrive as holidaymakers and leave as excess baggage and they aren't wrong.

Crackers

I ordered some prawn crackers over half an hour ago
to go with my mixed vegetables and rice
and grilled fish, and some paella
and diced chicken in white wine.
I thought a varied platter would be nice.

I've got lots of boiled potatoes with paprika
fried in oil
plus angel hair spaghetti on the side
and a heap of pickled cabbage, well you need the roughage, so
I just need my prawn crackers and I'm fine.

Should I risk the German meatballs
or would that be too much?
Oh just three or four won't hurt
they're only small.
And a bread roll for the gravy
now I see my plate is full.
I won't bother with prawn crackers after all.

Desserted

Shall I have a third dessert?
The answer should be "no".
Should I have a third dessert
or stagger up and go?
But something tells me there's still cake
and caramel ice cream
and chocolate curls, and more fresh fruit
this girl's living the dream.

Now I've had a third dessert
I'm feeling rather sick.
Oh look, here comes the chocolate torte
so I'll be leaving, quick.

***

OK, enough jollity, time for a rant. I feel very strongly about food waste, having been raised just after the war when food was scarce and precious. My mum would cook everything from scratch, so leaving anything at all was forbidden.

I couldn't believe the amount of lovely food left on plates while we were in Fuertaventura so I wrote this to express my disgust.

Doughnuts

Two fat and glistening doughnuts
one yellow and one pink
iced, and topped with sprinkles, on his plate.
The little boy stared long, but he made no attempt to eat.
Perhaps he wants to share them with his mate.

I got up to choose my dinner.
When I got back to my seat
the family had left, and lying there
two fat and glistening doughnuts
one yellow, and one pink
abandoned, left behind without a care.

The waitress looked disgusted as she cleared away his plate.
Two doughnuts she must throw into the bin.
And as she walked away I pondered sadly on their fate
for food waste is the ultimate in sin.

I thought of sad grey houses
where decisions must be made
heat or eat, go hungry or go cold
and the children bundled off to school
with a slice of bread and jam
for whom a fat iced doughnut would be gold.

I wish the boy who walked away
could know of them and think
before he left those doughnuts
one yellow and one pink.

***

I like to think of myself as a bit of a polyglot but when I try ordering food in a foreign tongue disaster inevitably ensues and I end up eating something I really didn't want in order to be polite.

Perhaps I should swallow my pride and just point at the pictures as my sensible husband does, although that wouldn't be half so much fun.

Lost in Translation

I'm not well versed in Spanish.
My German isn't great.
Which is why, instead of bacon
I have bratwurst on my plate.
I'm not a fan of bratwurst
it's difficult to chew
and if you're dentally challenged
it can be eventful too.

I'd love some almond croissants.
What the hell, give it a try.
But I don't have almond croissants
I have curried bratwurst.
Why?

This place is out to get me .
Of wurst I've had my fill.
So next year, bugger the Costas
we can holiday in Rhyl.

***

I put this poem in the food section as it was caused by over-indulgence at the festive season, a warning to all not to overload your plate.

The Christmas Onesie

I ordered a onesie for Christmas
to keep me warm at night.
It came in the post this morning
all sparkly, soft and white.
But oh, the zip, it won't zip up.
I must put myself on a fast.
The slip of a girl in a trim size ten
is the ghost of Christmas past.

***

A Poem for the Coronation

I don't really remember much about the coronation of Queen Elizabeth in 1953 as I was only three at the time, although I do remember lots of special cakes being made and my Auntie Ol bought a telly for the occasion, which was terribly exciting.

My family all squeezed into her cluttered front room (only used for special occasions) and peered at the tiny screen on which black and white figures moved through what looked like a snow storm.

This time we will be watching on our ancient John Lewis 1990s model (no new- fangled smart screen for us) but I did write this sparkly new verse for the occasion as I do feel a certain fondness for our royals, despite their faults.

The Lady in the Scarf is the poem I wrote for a competition set by the Suffolk Poetry Society. It describes the events around the coronation of King Charles as seen from the point of view of one of the Royal corgis.

I am very proud to say that I won a prize for this poem. It was put on a display board in Rushmere St Andrew as part of their Coronation celebrations and although I couldn't get there to see it and have my picture taken and generally show off like a fool, it remains the only prize I have ever won so I'm going to crow about it.

The lady in the scarf

Where is the lady in the scarf
who took me on my walks?
I miss her bright and sparkling eyes
our quiet, private talks.

She came to share her sorrow
when her husband passed away.
She stroked my fur and held me close
her friend, her faithful stay.
I miss my lady with the scarf
but my heart will swell with pride
to watch her son be crowned our king.
I will feel her by my side.

***

I have a good friend called Doris, the founder of the much missed Desperadoes, who is also a big fan of crochet.

She regularly yarn bombs her home town of Leiston with pillar box covers, flowers and all manner of jolly little pieces for people to find to gladden their days. The window at the pharmacy where she works is adorned with crocheted items like water bottles and pill boxes. It is much admired.

Recently Doris appeared in the local paper and on Suffolk radio due to her crochet as the street sign in her road had been badly damaged, the council weren't in a hurry to repair it, so she crocheted a replacement.

I loved this idea, and thought how nice it would be to have all the streets I had lived in (there are many) displayed in crochet form to mark the stages of my life. I was inspired to write this poem as a thank you to Doris for cheering up our world.

Crochet me a Life

Crochet me a life.
Crochet me a sign.
Crochet me a memory
of places that were mine.

4, Bury Cottages
Eastwoodbury Lane.
The place that held my childhood
where I cannot come again.

Crochet me a teenager
looking for her place.
Anxious, mixed up, angry
at 2, Warners Bridge Chase.

Crochet me a bride
living in Park Lane.
A tiny Southend attic flat
our shelter from the rain.

Crochet me a family
happy as we played
in swanky Earls Hall Avenue
sixteen years we stayed.

Crochet me an empty nest.
Children grown and gone.
Echoes bounce from silent walls.
Time for moving on.

Crochet me in Suffolk,
found where I belong.
To sing with friends, to write, to walk
to grow, and to be strong.

Crochet me the signposts
of each place I called my own.
To hold in loving memory
the people I have known.

***

In the town where I live, Saxmundham, there is a little café that opens every Wednesday for breakfasts and lunches.

It is a community space run by volunteers and staffed by people with learning difficulties, who are always cheerful and lit up by pride in their work.

The manager, Tom, kept asking me to write a poem about the café, which is called Smile. As it is a small friendly space I wrote a small, simple poem which I hope captures the special atmosphere of our Wednesday morning treat.

Smile

Fish finger baps at the Smile café
Wednesday morning, if we're free.
With tartare sauce, and a cup of tea.

Humming with chat at the Smile café
Wednesday morning, if we're free.
Dogs to pat, friends to see.

News to impart at the Smile café
Wednesday morning, if we're free.
Gossipers love company.

Come and sit down at the Smile café
Wednesday morning, if you're free.
Come and chat with me.

Rants

I always enjoy a good rant, it makes me feel better when life just poos on you from on high, and hopefully you will enjoy them. These may be first world problems but they can be so damned annoying and I am sure you could add your own to my list. Let me know and I'll write a little poem for you.

I sometimes sell my books and my handmade jewellery at little craft fairs around Suffolk but recently I decided to be more ambitious and booked an outside table for the day at a local music festival. "Bring your own gazebo and table" they said so undaunted we ordered one from ebay and it arrived promptly the next day. Unfortunately we were out at the time so they left it in the garden, it rained heavily and the box was ruined.

Never mind, we unpacked the contents, gasped at the amount of poles and the length and complexity of the instructions, and I left my husband to it with the promise of help if needed.

Much later that afternoon I peeped out to witness a scene of devastation. Our tiny garden was festooned with poles, my husband's face held a wild expression and the instructions lay crumpled at his feet. We never did erect our gazebo, I sold it a few days later and cancelled my booking with the festival, losing my deposit and my pride but relieved that our struggles were over. Indoor events for us from now on. I did however have this fine verse to warn others not to emulate my folly and imagine skills they do not possess.

The Gazebo Poem

Bring a gazebo for your stall.
Ok, no probs, will do.
Lots up on ebay really cheap.
Quick to assemble too.

He's been gone an hour, all I see
Are poles strewn on the ground.
He swears, he stamps, he's losing it.
I'll help him, I'm not proud.

The damned gazebo's six feet high.
I'm only five foot one.
We haven't got a ladder.
I am not having fun.

Should they say "Provide your own marquee"
You tell them where to go.
Ask if they have an indoor pitch
And if they don't, say no.

***

While I am in the mood for a good rant here's one I wrote one wet day when everything seemed to be going wrong and then a cheery missive dropped onto the mat to add to the general despair.

Road Rage

We drove our car through Maldon
We didn't want to go
But the old A12 was all closed off
So the traffic couldn't flow.

We strayed into a bus lane
Apparently we did.
We had a letter telling us
It's cost us thirty quid.

We didn't want to go there
We won't go there again.
We're staying here in Suffolk
And sulking, in the rain.

***

I really wanted to see the Aldeburgh Carnival, our friends said it was an event not to be missed so, not wanting to add to the traffic chaos and being a big fan of local buses, we caught the 11.15 and arrived in Aldeburgh very excited, despite the fact that the town was closed off and we had a 20 minute uphill walk in the sweltering heat before we reached the action.

We were informed the last bus left at 5.50. Then we found the carnival started at 3.45 and if we stayed to watch it we wouldn't be able to get home.

Disappointed, we left at 2.30 only to find we had been misinformed about the timetable and would have to wait nearly an hour for the next bus.

On the journey back we shared the hot, crowded space with a family who swore loudly and explicitly at their unfortunate children. This added to the general gloom and so I wrote this verse to express my disgust with people who do this, it's horrible for everyone around them as well as their poor offspring.

Mind Your Language

Kind parents, don't swear at your children
If you want them to behave.
Don't sit on the bus and curse them and cuss
Like Neanderthals deep in your cave.

It won't turn them into nice people
They'll hate you and never forget
Those cruel ugly words
Not fit for the birds.
They'll repeat them all!

That's what you'll get.

I don't want to imbibe your foul language
I'm tired and thirsty and hot.
As I sit by the door on the red 64
And sadly reflect on my lot.

I came to the Aldeburgh Carnival
Left the car safely at home.
Well I wish that we'd brought it
Or that you'd been taught it's
More wise to leave cross kids alone.

Oh don't swear at your kids on the bus please

Or keep your voice down if you do.
For if you continue to make such a din you
May find I'll start swearing at you.

Thanks

I have many people to thank for helping me to produce this little collection of poems:

My patient and supportive husband for solving my technical problems and finding my files when I insisted on deleting them.

The Fram Friends for inspiration, encouragement and cake.
Ruth Leigh and Mai Black whose encouragement and advice have been so valuable.

Most of all to the Suffolk Writers' Group for your wisdom and humour, without you I would have given up for sure.

***

Printed in Great Britain
by Amazon